This Book Belongs To

_____

Contents

- Savoury Chicken Traybake
- Chicken Fried Rice
- Toad in the Hole
- Tomato & Red Pepper Sauce for Pasta
- Chili con Carne
- Cauliflower Cheese
- French Onion Soup
- Carib-Asian Roast Chicken
- Hasselback Potatoes
- Ultimate Chicken Pie
- Chicken Chow Mein
- Chicken & Chickpea Curry
- Chinese Chili Oil
- Healthy Chinese Chicken Broth
- Crispy Chili Beef
- Katsu Chicken Curry Soup
- How to Brine a Chicken
- Chinese Char Sui Pork
- Tomato & Basil Soup
- Christmas Brussels
- Steak with Peppercorn Sauce
- Christmassy Sausage Rolls
- Spicy BBQ Wings
- Chinese BBQ Ribs
- Sweet & Sour King Prawns
- Blueberry Muffins
- Lemon Drizzle
- Banana Muffins
- Apple Tarte Tatin
- Self Saucing Chocolate Pudding
- Quick 5 min Sponge
- Waffles & Blueberry Syrup
- Apple Crumble Cake
- Kettle Corn/Popcorn
- Mince Pie Crumble Bars
- Amazing Chocolate Brownies
- Best Ever Carrot Cake Muffins
- Blueberry Filo Pastry Pie
- Sticky Toffee Pudding

Copyright © 2024 Maria Keenan
All rights reserved. No part of this book may be
reproduced in any form without written permission of
the author.

I Love Food

I mean, who doesn't!

I wanted to create a simple cookbook for anyone that wants to cook but may feel intimidated and doesn't quite know where to start. Here are my favourite recipes which anyone can make and love. And may just ignite your fire for cooking!

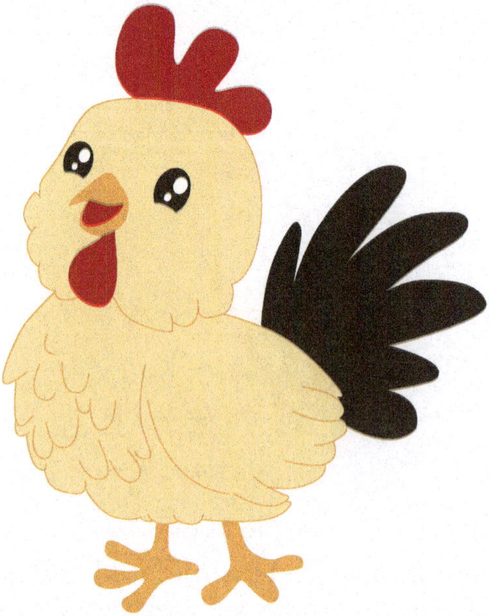

Savoury Chicken Tray Bake

Ingredients

1 onion red or white
1 table spoon olive oil
3-4 cloves garlic
2 red peppers chopped
1/2 bag new potatoes
1 carrot chopped
4 chicken thighs - bone & skin on
1/2 jar sun dried red pesto
150g cherry tomatoes
squirt of tomato puree
1 tablespoon mixed herbs
salt & pepper

Method

Boil potatoes and carrots for 10 mins
Add all ingredients into a baking dish with the chicken on top (skin side up)
Cover with foil
Pop in oven for 30 mins at 200.c
Remove foil and cook for another 15-20 mins or until chicken is brown and skin crispy

#ENJOY

Chicken Fried Rice

Ingredients

1 small onion chopped
2 tablespoons vegetable oil
2 garlic cloves chopped or grated
1" ginger chopped or grated
1/2 sweetheart cabbage
2 cups day old steamed rice
3 eggs, 1 cup chopped cooked chicken
1/2 cup frozen peas
2 tablespoon oyster sauce
2 tablespoon light soy sauce
1/2-1 teaspoon white pepper

Method

Add sesame oil, onion & cabbage to a frying pan over a med high heat.
Fry for about 5 -10 mins until soft.
Add garlic and ginger and fry for 2 mins.
Add the cooked rice and mix.
Push to one side and add 3 eggs to scramble in pan.
Once done, add chicken and frozen peas. Cook for 5 mins
Add oyster sauce, soy sauce & white pepper.

Variations - add prawns

#ENJOY

Toad in the Hole

Ingredients

1 pack of 8 sausages
2 tablespoons vegetable oil

Batter

4oz plain flour, pinch salt
3 eggs
250ml milk

Method

Preheat oven to 200.c
Add sausages and oil into an oven proof dish. Cook until sausages start to brown slightly - approx 15 mins

Meanwhile whisk all of the batter ingredients together in a bowl/jug then leave to one side.
Then add the batter mix quickly into the sausages and return to the oven immediately.
Cook for about 20-30 mins until the batter has risen and is golden brown.

Serve with mashed potato, onion gravy or baked beans!

#ENJOY

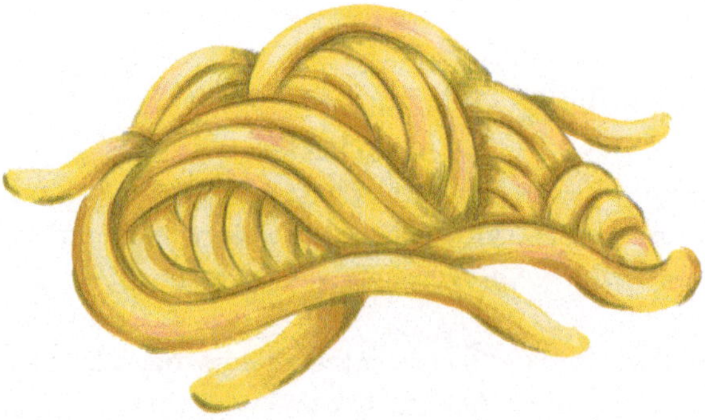

Tomato & Red Pepper Sauce for Pasta

Ingredients

1 onion chopped
1 tablespoon olive oil
2 tins plum tomatoes - blended or chopped
300g jar of roasted red peppers - blitz in the food processor
4 cloves garlic chopped or grated
50g tomato puree
1 teaspoon worcestershire sauce
1 tablespoon mixed herbs
1/2 - 1 tablespoon sugar

Method

Fry the onion in the oil then add the garlic.
Blitz the tomatoes and red peppers incl liquid in a blender.
Add in all of the remaining ingredients and simmer for 20-30 mins.
Either serve on pasta with grated cheese or add to browned mince for a tasty bolognaise.

#ENJOY

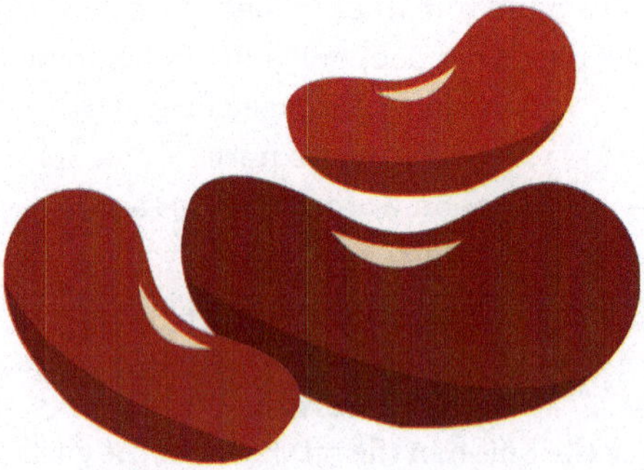

Chili con Carne

Ingredients
500g lean beef mince
2 garlic cloves chopped or grated
1 tablespoon olive oil
1 onion chopped, 1-2 beef oxo cube
2 tablespoons ground cumin
1 tablespoon sugar
1 tablespoon smoked paprika
1/2 - 1 teaspoon cayenne pepper
1 400g tin plum or chopped tomatoes
1 400g tin kidney beans in chili sauce
1 cinnamon stick
squirt of tomato puree
Salt & pepper, 1/2 teaspoon chili flakes

Method
Fry the onion in the oil for a few mins.
Add the mince and fry for 5 mins then add the garlic.
Add the oxo cube, cumin, sugar, paprika, cayenne & fry for 2 mins.
Add in tomatoes, chili beans, tomato puree, salt & pepper, chili and cinnamon stick.
Mix then simmer for 30 mins stirring occasionally.

Serve with steamed rice and top with grated cheddar.

#ENJOY

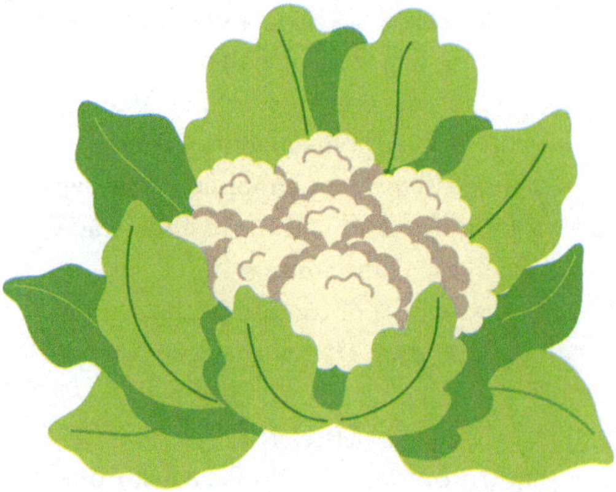

Cauliflower Cheese

Ingredients

70g plain flour
70g butter
700ml milk
1 large cauliflower
1 tablespoon dijon mustard
Salt & Pepper, 1-2 cups of grated mature cheese

Method

Parboil the cauliflower then put into an ovenproof dish.
Put the flour, butter & milk into a saucepan and melt on low/med heat.
Once butter has melted turn up heat slightly and use a whisk as it will thicken quickly.
Once it starts to bubble you can turn off the heat.
Add the mustard, salt & pepper & half of the grated cheese.
Stir and pour on top of the cauliflower.
Add the remaining cheese on top.
Cover with foil and bake for 20-30 mins.
Remove foil and bake for another 20 mins until golden brown.

You can also add cooked pasta or salmon & peas to this to make a full meal.

#ENJOY

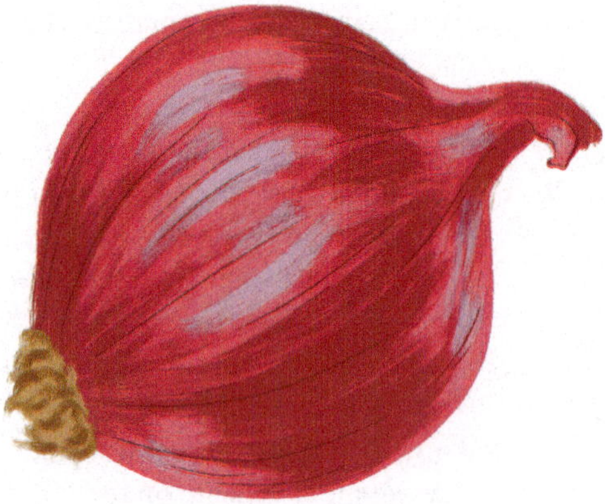

French Onion Soup

Ingredients

5 onions sliced thinly
2 tablespoons olive oil
1 tablespoon granulated sugar
2 tablespoons plain flour
3 cloves of garlic chopped or grated
200ml white wine
1 pint of water.
4 beef oxo cubes
1 bay leaf
1 garlic bread stick
1 cup of grated cheddar/mozzarella

Method

Fry onions in the oil for 10-15 mins or until soft and brown.
Add the sugar.
Cover and cook on low/medium heat for 30 -60 mins
Add the garlic & flour & cook for a minute.
Add the wine and bring to the boil for 2 mins.
Add the water, Oxo & bayleaf. Season with salt & pepper.
Bring to the boil and simmer for 5 mins. Put into individual dishes.
Top with toasted garlic bread slices.
Top with the cheese.
Put into a preheated oven 200.c for 5 mins until the cheese has melted.

#ENJOY

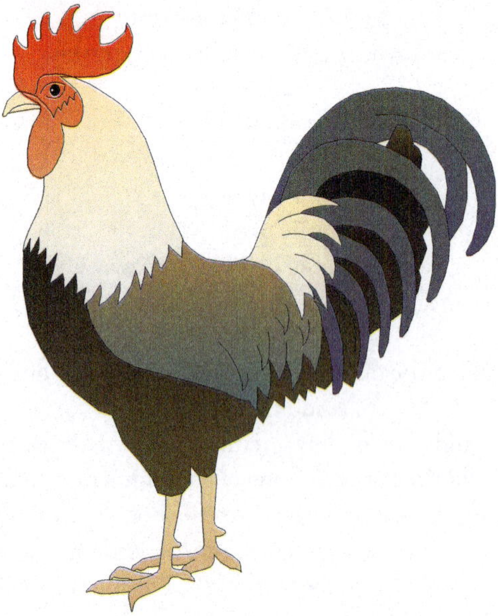

My Carib-Asian Chicken

Ingredients
1 whole chicken
1 tablespoon all purpose seasoning
1 tablespoon paprika
1 teaspoon 5 spice powder
1/4 teaspoon nutmeg
1/4 teaspoon cayenne pepper
1 tablespoon olive oil
1 lemon, 1 onion

Method
Combine all of the dry ingredients and the olive oil.
Rub all over the chicken
Cut the lemon and onion in half and stuff inside the chicken.
Put on a baking dish and cover with foil.
Cook in a preheated oven at 200.c for approx. 45 mins.
Uncover and then cook for a further 30 mins or until cooked.

Serve with salad and a Hassel back potato.

#ENJOY

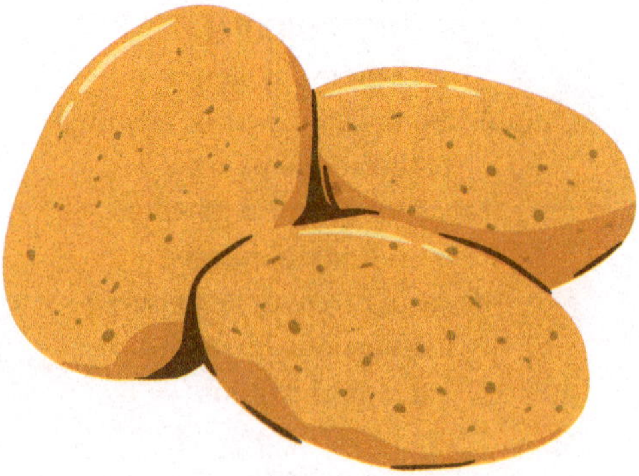

Hasselback Potatoes

Ingredients
4 large baking potatoes
2 tablespoons of olive oil
200g butter
1 onion sliced
200g grated cheddar
Salt & pepper

Method
Parboil the potatoes for 5 minutes.
Cover the potatoes with the olive oil
Make cuts all along each potato but don't go all the way through.
Between each cut add a slice of butter, onion and cheese.
Top with salt & pepper

Put into a baking dish and cover with foil.
Put into a preheated oven of 200.c for 45 mins.
Remove foil and cook for a further 20 mins until brown and cooked through.

#ENJOY

My Ultimate Chicken Pie

Ingredients

1 onion chopped
1 tablespoon olive oil
2 chicken breasts chopped
50g plain flour
50g butter
500ml milk
1 teaspoon Dijon mustard
Salt & pepper
2 bay leaves
1 chicken oxo cube
1/2 teaspoon dried thyme.
2 carrots, 1/2 head broccoli
1 small can sweetcorn
1/4 cup frozen peas
1 packet of ready rolled puff pastry

Method

Fry onion in the oil. Add the chicken & fry for 2-3 mins.
Add the flour and stir in. Then add the butter, milk & Dijon.
Bring to a boil and keep stirring, then turn down to a simmer.
Add salt & pepper, bay leaves and 1 oxo cube.
Add the cooked carrots & broccoli, frozen peas and can of sweetcorn.
Tip into an oven proof dish.
Top with the whole roll of puff pastry, tucking in the edges.
Brush over with milk and use a knife to make cuts all over the pastry.
Bake in a preheated oven at 200.c for 30 mins or until pastry has puffed up and golden brown.

#ENJOY

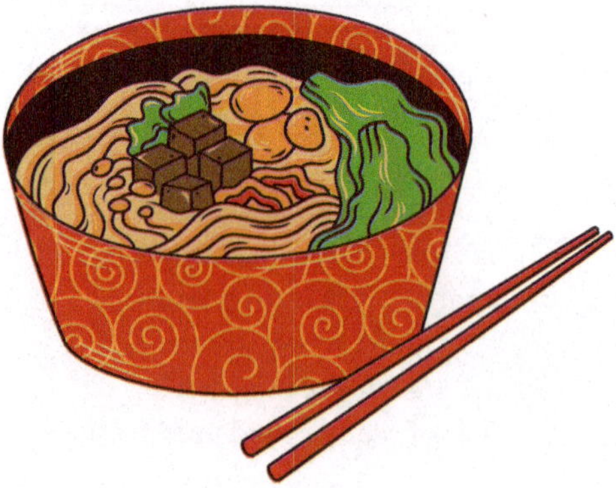

Chicken Chow Mein

Ingredients

4 nests of medium egg noodles
(boiled for 2-3 mins & rinsed in cold water)
1 tablespoon dark soy
2 Tablespoon light soy
1 tablespoon sesame oil
1 Tablespoon sugar
1 small chili chopped
1-2 tablespoons oyster sauce
2 tablespoon veg oil
3 tablespoons water
1" piece of ginger chopped
3 garlic cloves chopped
1/2 green pepper
1/2 red pepper
1 pack bean sprouts
1 pack tender stem broccoli
1/2 sweetheart cabbage sliced thinly. 1/2 onion
2 chicken breasts sliced and chopped
2 eggs

Method

Add 1 tablespoon of veg oil to a pan and fry the onion, ginger, garlic & chili for a few mins. Add the chicken and fry till cooked. Add 2 eggs and scramble. Remove both and set aside.
Add 1 tablespoon of oil to the pan and add the veggies except the beansprouts. Fry for 5 mins or until cooked to your liking. Finally add noodles, beansprouts and chicken/egg and sesame oil.
Stir and cook for 2 mins to heat through then serve.
Taste and add more soy sauce and top with chili oil if required.

#ENJOY

Chicken & Chickpea Curry

Ingredients

6 chicken thighs bone in
1 tin chickpeas - drained
3 tablespoons olive oil
1 onion sliced
1/2 tin chopped tomatoes
1 can coconut milk
2 teaspoons salt
2 teaspoons sugar
2 garlic cloves
1" ginger both grated

spice blend

1 teaspoon turmeric
1 tablespoon coriander
1 tablespoon cumin
2 tablespoons garam masala
1 tablespoon mild curry powder
1-2 teaspoons mild chili powder
1/2 can water
1 cup of mushrooms chopped

Method

Fry onions in the oil on a medium high heat for a few minutes.
Then add the ginger & garlic and fry for 2 mins.
Now add the spices and fry for 2 mins.
Add the tomatoes and water, salt & sugar - stir.
Then add the chicken, chickpeas & mushrooms.
Simmer for 30 mins with the lid off.
Add a cup of peas and simmer for 5 mins.

#ENJOY

Chinese Chili Oil

Ingredients
1 cup red chili flakes
1 cup vegetable or any flavourless oil
3 garlic cloves chopped or grated
2" piece of garlic sliced
1.5 teaspoon salt
1 teaspoon sugar
1 cinnamon stick
3 cloves

Method
Put the chili flakes, garlic, salt & sugar into a bowl.
Put the oil into a saucepan and heat to 250.f
Add the cinnamon, cloves & ginger and simmer for 20 mins

Remove aromatics and heat to 350.f
Pour oil onto the chili flakes and stir.
Pour into a sterilised jar.
Will keep for 6 months refrigerated.

#ENJOY

Healthy Chinese Chicken Broth

Ingredients
1 tablespoon veg oil
3 chopped chicken thighs
2 chopped garlic cloves
2" piece of ginger chopped
1 chopped green chili,
200ml water or chicken stock
1 teaspoon Shaoxing rice wine
1 tablespoon soy sauce
1/2-1 tablespoon chicken bouillon
1/4 teaspoon white pepper
1/2 chopped chinese leaf
1/2 pack of French green beans
1 tablespoon oyster sauce
2 spring onions chopped
1 tablespoon sesame oil

Method
Put the oil in a pan and add the chicken, garlic, chili & ginger.
Fry for 5 mins or until chicken is cooked.
Add the remaining ingredients and simmer for 10 mins.
Ladle over freshly steamed rice.

#ENJOY

Chinese Crispy Chili Beef with a Simple Asian Salad

Ingredients:

Salad

1 large carrot cut into fine julienne
1/2 cucumber cut into fine julienne
1/2 green/red pepper cut into fine julienne
1 tablespoon sugar, 2 tablespoons rice vinegar, 1 clove garlic grated, 1 red chili chopped
1 tablespoon sesame oil, 1 tablespoon fish sauce, 1 tablespoon lemon/lime juice

2 steaks of your choice sliced thinly
1/2 cup cornflour, 1 egg
2 tablespoons ketchup, sweet chili sauce
1 teaspoon dark soy sauce, 1 tablespoon light soy
2 tablespoon rice vinegar
1 tablespoon brown sugar
1 red or green chili or 1/2 teaspoon chili flakes

Method

Combine carrot/cucumber/pepper with sugar, vinegar, garlic, chili, sesame oil, fish sauce, lemon/lime juice. Set to one side.

Mix steak with egg & cornflower. Add to hot oil individually & shallow fry on a high heat for approx 4-5 mins. Remove and set aside.

Fry the onion and red pepper for 3-4 mins.
Then add the ketchup, sweet chili, soy, vinegar, sugar, chili
Heat till bubbling

Serve with the simple salad or with steamed rice.

#ENJOY

My Pret Katsu Chicken Curry Soup

Ingredients

1 tablespoon veg oil, 1 celery stick,
1/2 onion chopped
1 chili, 1" ginger, 2 cloves garlic chopped
1 tablespoon curry powder
1 teaspoon turmeric
500ml water
2 chicken oxo cubes
100g fresh tomatoes chopped
1 large potato chopped
200g butternut squash chopped
1 large cooked chicken breast chopped
1 tablespoon light soy sauce
1 400g tin coconut milk
Salt & Pepper to taste, 1 tablespoon lemon juice
1 teaspoon vegetable bouillon
100g cooked brown rice, 1/2 cup frozen peas

My Katsu Chicken Curry Soup continued..

Method

Add oil, celery, onion to a pan & fry for 2-3 mins.
Add the chili, ginger, garlic, fry for 1 min
Then add the curry powder & turmeric & fry for 1 min.
Add the water and Oxo, tomatoes then blend with hand blender.
Then add the potato, butternut squash & chicken, soy sauce and simmer for 10 mins.
Add the coconut milk, salt & pepper, lemon juice, bouillon & rice.
Once potatoes and squash are cooked add in the peas and simmer for 2-3 mins.

Serve as is or with a side of garlic bread
#ENJOY

How to Brine a Chicken

Ingredients

1 chicken
3 pints water
1 tablespoon sugar
1 tablespoon salt
1 tablespoon star anise
4 cloves, 10 black peppercorns
2 bay leaves
1/2 lemon
2 tangerines or 1 orange
1/2 onion

Method

Add all ingredients and warm gently just enough to dissolve the sugar & salt then leave to cool.
Add your chicken to the pan of brine and leave in a fridge covered overnight.
When ready to cook the next day, drain off the brine and disguard.
Add chicken to a pan and cover with foil.
Bake at 180 for 45 mins, then remove foil and cook for a further 30 mins until brown and crispy. Time may vary depending upon the size of your chicken.

Serve with a salad or roast potatoes and all the trimmings.

#ENJOY

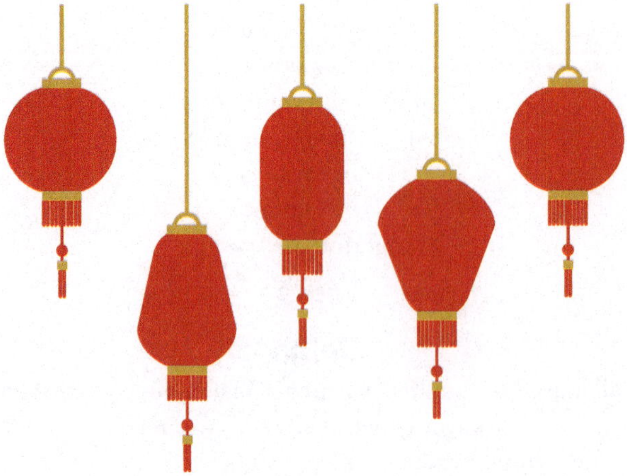

Chinese Char Sui Pork

Ingredients

1kg pork shoulder slice in half lengthways
1 1/2 tablespoons brown sugar
1/4 cup honey
1/4 cup hoisin sauce
3 tablespoons light soy sauce
1 teaspoon 5 spice
1 tablespoon vegetable oil

Method

Mix all ingredients together and pour over pork shoulder.
Place into a dish or Ziploc bag and leave overnight or up to 48hrs.

Place meat onto a rack above a roasting tin/tray and cook for 30 mins at 160.c
Put remaining marinade into a saucepan and cook until syrupy.
Use this to glaze the meat then back in the oven for another 30 mins.
Reglaze then back in the oven again for 20 mins.
Leave to rest for 20 mins before slicing thinly.

#ENJOY

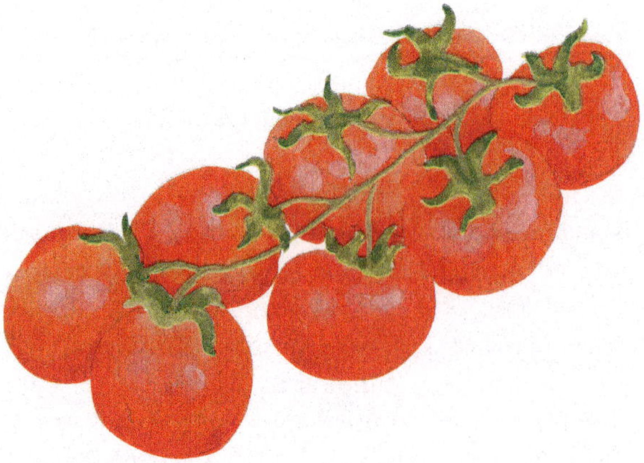

Tomato & Basil Soup

Ingredients
1 tablespoon olive oil
1 onion chopped
2 cloves garlic chopped
1 celery stick chopped
1 carrot chopped
2 tins tomatoes
1/2 jar roasted red peppers incl liquid
1 tin water
1 tablespoon Worcestershire sauce
2 -3 tablespoons sugar
1-2 tablespoons tomato puree
handful of basil leaves

Method
Add the olive oil to a saucepan.
Add the onion, carrot, celery and fry for 5 mins. Add the garlic and fry for a further 2 mins.
Add the remaining ingredients except for the basil and simmer for 20 mins.
Then add the basil leaves and blend to your desired consistency.
Serve with a cheese toastie!

#ENJOY

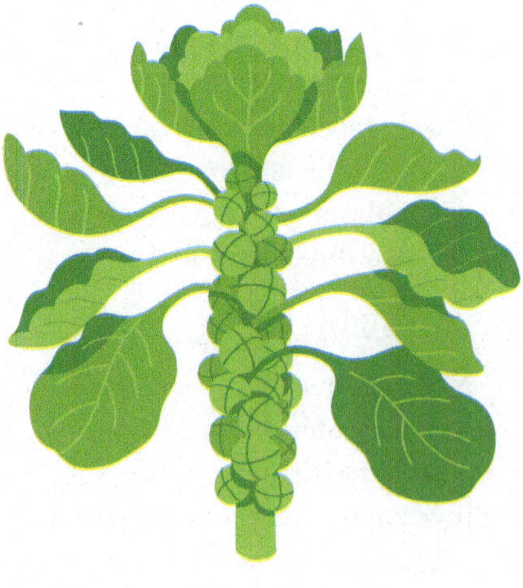

Christmas Brussels

Ingredients
1 pack of Brussel sprouts peeled and halved
1/2 onion chopped
1 tablespoon olive oil
1 teaspoon wholegrain mustard
250ml single cream
1/4 cup white wine
1/4 cup grated cheddar
Salt & pepper

Method
Add the oil and onion to a pan and fry for 2 mins.
Add the sprouts and fry for 5-10 mins on a medium heat with the lid on but stirring regularly.
Add the white wine and cook for 2 mins.
Add the cream and mustard, salt & pepper to taste.
Cook for 2/3 mins then add to a dish.
Sprinkle the top with the cheddar and cover with foil.
Bake in a preheated oven of 180.c for 20 mins.
Remove the foil and cook for a further 10 mins.

#ENJOY

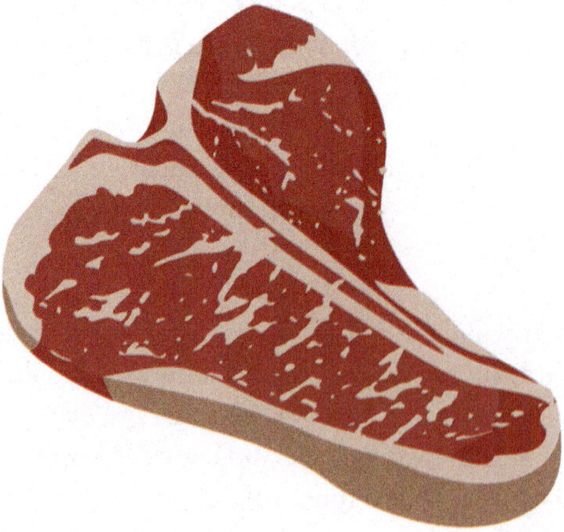

Steak with Peppercorn Sauce

Ingredients

2 steaks of your choice
1 onion sliced, 1 beef oxo cube
1-2 tablespoons brandy
1 teaspoon Dijon mustard
270ml carton single cream
1 tablespoon oil
1/2-1 tablespoon crushed black pepper(depending upon your taste)
Salt & pepper

Method

Add oil and onions to a med/high heat and fry till soft & have a good color.
Remove and keep warm
Add the steaks and cook to your liking then remove to a plate and cover with foil to keep warm.
Return the onions to the pan. Add the brandy to the pan and flambe. When flames have disappeared add the cream, oxo, Dijon and salt & peppercorns. Simmer for 3-4 mins.

Serve with chips and peas or your choice of side.

#ENJOY

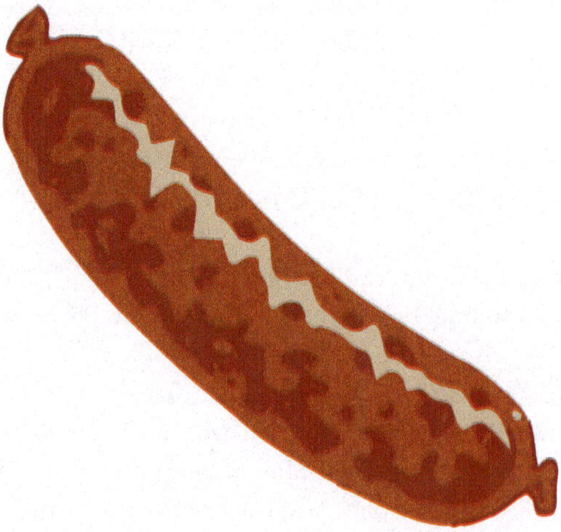

Christmassy Sausage Rolls

Ingredients
1 pack of ready rolled puff pastry
1 pack of sausage meat or pack of 8 sausages
Cranberry sauce
Brie
Sesame seeds

Method
Unroll your pasty and cut in half lengthways.
Shape your sausagemeat so it fits all along one length.
Spread several teaspoons of cranberry along the sausagemeat.
Add brie slices along the top.
Put the remaining slice of pasty on top and press the edges together.
Cut into approx. 1 1/2" sections and place onto a baking tray.
Egg wash the tops and sprinkle with sesame seeds.
Bake at 200.c for about 20 mins or until nicely browned.

#ENJOY

JUST WING IT

Spicy BBQ Chicken Wings

Ingredients

1kg chicken wings, 1/4 cup soy sauce
1/4 cup rice vinegar, 1 teaspoon black pepper
1/2 tablespoon paprika, 3 garlic cloves chopped

Sauce

1/4 cup ketchup
1/4 cup brown sauce
1/4 cup brown sugar
1/4 cup honey
1/4 teaspoon chili flakes
1 teaspoon Worcestershire sauce
1/4 cup soy sauce

Method

Combine marinade and pour over wings and leave for 6-12hrs
Air fry for 15-20 mins approx.
Combine sauce ingredients in a saucepan and bring to the boil. Simmer for 5 mins then pour over the wings.
(add a tablespoon of water if too thick)

#ENJOY

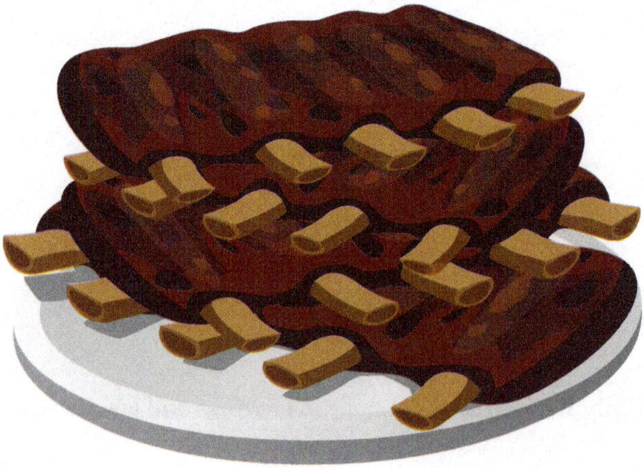

Chinese BBQ Ribs

Ingredients

1 pack of meaty pork ribs
2 tablespoons hoisin sauce
2 tablespoon yellowbean sauce
3-4 cloves of garlic chopped
1 teaspoon garlic granules
1/2 chopped onion
2 tablespoons tomato puree
1/2 cup brown sugar
1/2 tablespoon 5 spice
1 cinnamon stick
1-2 star anise
1 teaspoon salt
1 tablespoon Shaoxing rice wine

Method

Throw all of the ingredients into a large pan and add just enough water to almost cover the ribs.
Bring to the boil and simmer for 1 1/2 hours
Remove the ribs and airfry for 5 mins or so.
Strain the remaining liquid and reduce until slightly thick. Add 1 teaspoon cornflour to make a slurry and add to the sauce to thicken slightly.
Pour over the ribs.

#ENJOY

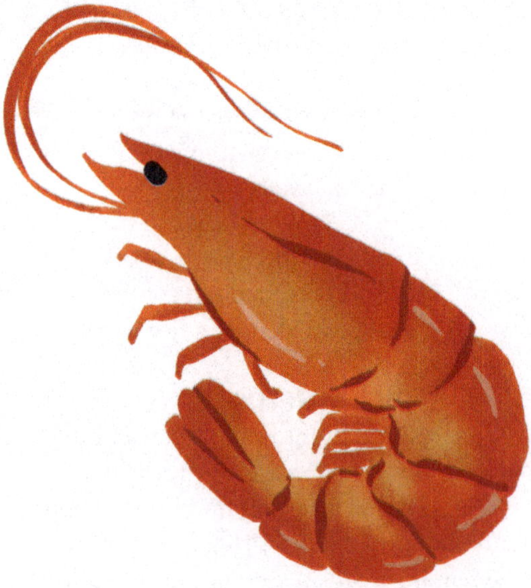

Sweet & Sour King Prawns

Ingredients

10 king prawns
1 egg
2-3 tablespoons cornflour
1/2 red pepper sliced
1/2 green pepper sliced
1/2 onion sliced

1 tablespoon ketchup
2 tablespoons soy sauce
3 tablespoons sugar
4 tablespoons white vinegar
3 tablespoons water

Method

Mix the prawns with the egg and cornflour and deep fry till golden brown. Remove and place on paper towel.

Put all of the remaining ingredients into a pan and bring to the boil.
Reduce until the sauce has thickened to your preference. Should be done in about 4-5 mins.
You can add the peppers/onion in the last few minutes if you prefer them to be crunchy.
Finally pour the sauce over the crispy prawns.

#ENJOY

Sweet Treats

We all need these in our lives

Best Blueberry Muffins

Ingredients
2 cups plain flour
2 teaspoons baking powder
1/2 teaspoon salt
1 & 1/4 cup sugar
8 tablespoons melted butter (112g)
2 eggs
2 teaspoons vanilla extract
1/2 cup milk
1 cup blueberries

Syrup
1 cup blueberries
1 tablespoon lemon juice
1 tablespoon granulated sugar

3 tablespoons of any streusel/crumble topping (butter, flour, sugar, oats)

Method
Add the 1 cup of blueberries, lemon juice & sugar in a saucepan and bring to the boil and simmer for 5 mins until jammy.

In a bowl mix all of the dry ingredients. In a separate bowl mix all of the wet ingredients. Mix the two together until just combined.
Spoon into 10 lined muffin cases leaving the 2 middle holes empty.
Add a spoon of the blueberry syrup and a spoon of the crumble mix onto each muffin. Add 1cm of water in the 2 middle empty tins.
This stops them drying out during baking.
Bake at 210.c for 10 mins then lower the temp to 180.c and bake for a further 10-15 mins until risen and a toothpick comes out clean.

#ENJOY

Lemon Drizzle

Ingredients
4oz self raising flour
1 teaspoon baking powder
4oz granulated sugar
4oz any spread (Flora, Olive etc)
2 medium eggs, zest of 1 lemon
1 tablespoon of milk

Juice of 1/2 lemon
2oz granulated sugar

Method
Put the spread and sugar into microwavable bowl and blast on high for 20 seconds & mix.
Add the eggs, flour, baking powder, zest from 1 lemon, milk and beat for about
30 seconds to 1 min.
Put into a small lined loaf tin and bake at 170.c for 25-30 mins or until toothpick/skewer comes out clean.
Mix the lemon juice and 2oz sugar together.
Poke hole with skewer all over the top and add the *extra sugar with the lemon juice mix* all over the top.
Leave in the tin to cool.

#ENJOY

Banana Muffins

Ingredients

140g butter softened
120g sugar
2 ripe bananas mashed
2 eggs

1 teaspoon cinnamon
175g self raising flour
1 teaspoon bicarbonate of soda
1 teaspoon baking powder
1/4 cup chopped walnuts

Method

Beat the butter then add the sugar and beat.
Add the eggs one at a time then add the bananas beating between each one.
Fold in the flour, bicarb, baking powder, cinnamon & walnuts.
Divide the mixture into 8-9 muffin cases.
Bake at 200.c for 10 mins then 180.c for a further 10 mins.

#ENJOY

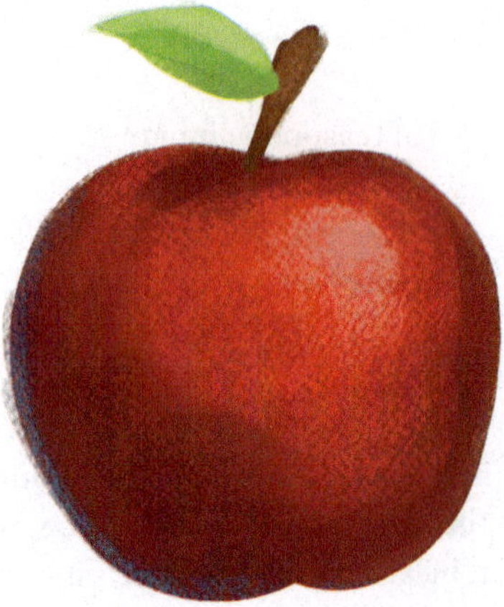

Apple Tarte Tatin

Ingredients
4 apples peeled, cored and sliced into large chunks
100g sugar
80g unsalted butter
1 pack of ready rolled puff pastry

Method
Put the butter and sugar into a round pie dish
Place in a preheated oven at 200.c for 10 mins until melted.
Arrange the apples into a circle pattern in the hot butter & sugar dish.
Return to the oven for about 20mins until caramelised or starting to brown.
Put the pastry on top of the apples, tucking in the edges.
Place back into the oven for about 20-30 mins or until the pastry is golden brown and take out of the oven.
Place a large plate on top of the pastry and flip over.
Remove the pie dish and voila.
Cool for 5 mins before slicing.
Serve with vanilla ice-cream

#ENJOY

Chocolate Self-Saucing Pudding

Ingredients

150g plain flour
2 1/2 teaspoons baking powder
70g granulated sugar
30g cocoa powder
pinch of salt
1 teaspoon vanilla extract
50g melted butter
1 egg, 125ml milk
150g drinking chocolate & 50g sugar
1 1/4 cups boiling water

Method

Preheat oven to 150.c
Put dry ingredients into a bowl.
Put butter, egg, vanilla into a separate bowl and whisk.
Combine the 2 bowls and put into a greased oven proof dish.
Sprinkle on the drinking chocolate/sugar mixture.
Pour on the boiling water.
Place in the oven.
Bake for 30 mins or until top has formed a crust like topping.
Serve with vanilla ice cream.

#ENJOY

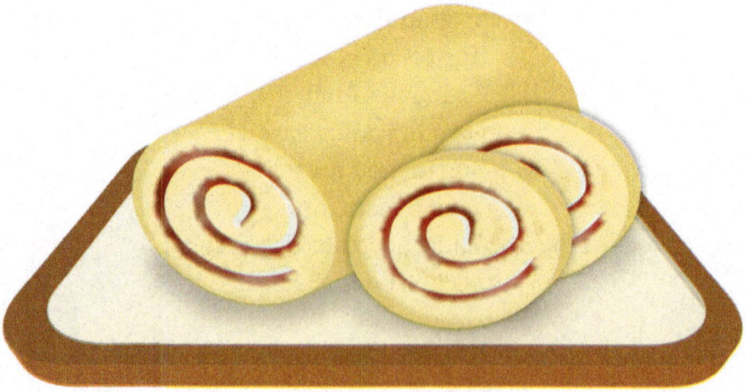

5 Minute Sponge Pudding

Ingredients
4oz self raising flour
1 teaspoon baking powder
4oz baking spread
4oz sugar
2 eggs
Zest of 1/2 lemon & 1-2 tablespoons milk
Golden syrup

Method
Mix all of the ingredients together except for the golden syrup.
Put in a glass dish.
Microwave on high for 4 mins

Serve with golden syrup and hot custard
(You can add the syrup in the dish before the batter if you prefer)

You can also omit the lemon zest and add in 1oz of cocoa powder for a chocolate sponge option.

#ENJOY

Waffles & Blueberry Syrup

Ingredients
250g plain flour
1 teaspoon baking powder
20g sugar
pinch of salt
475ml milk
30ml vegetable oil, 2 eggs

Syrup
125g blueberries
1 teaspoon cornflour
1/2 cup sugar
1/2 cup cold water
1 teaspoon lemon juice

Method
Put all of the syrup ingredients into a saucepan and bring to the boil. Simmer for 5 mins - keep stirring - crush some of the berries. Set aside.

Put dry ingredients into a bowl
Put wet ingredients into a separate bowl
Mix both together until just combined. There will be lumps.
Once heated to temperature, lightly spray oil onto your waffle irons.
Add enough mix for your machine. Cook as desired.
Serve topped with the blueberry syrup or add ice cream for an evening dessert!

#ENJOY

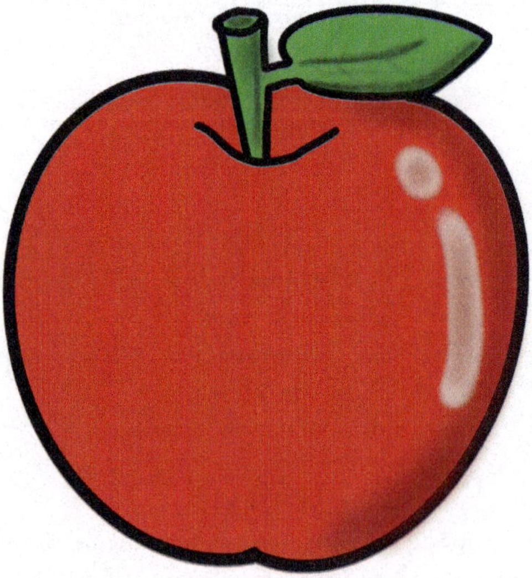

Apple & Blueberry Crumble Cake

Ingredients

2 cups self raising flour
1 teaspoon baking powder
1 cup sugar
1 cup milk
2 eggs, 1 teaspoon vanilla extract
1/2 cup melted butter
3 apples peeled & chopped
1 cup blueberries

For the crumble mix
1/2 cup oats, 1/2 cup flour
1/2 cup desiccated coconut, 1/2 cup brown sugar
1/2 cup melted butter

Method

Add the flour, baking powder, sugar, milk butter eggs, vanilla to a bowl and mix. Add the apples and blueberries & mix.
Pour into a lined baking tin 8" deep.

Mix all of the crumble ingredients and springle on top of the batter. I used 2/3 of the crumble mix and saved the rest in the freezer.
Bake 170.c for 45-55 mins or until skewer comes out clean.
Perfect hot with custard.

#ENJOY

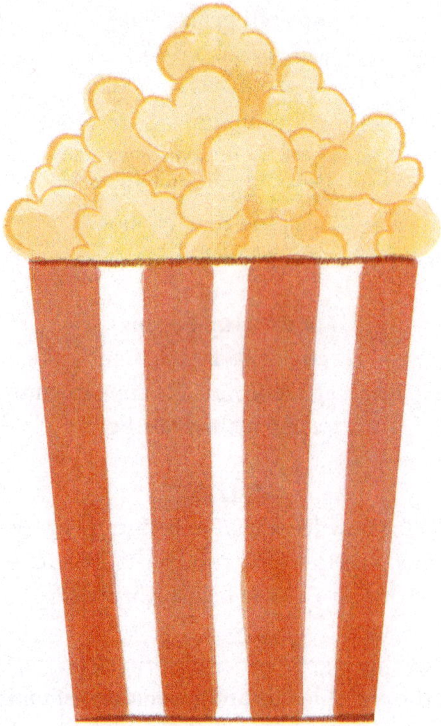

Popcorn /Kettlecorn

Ingredients
1/2 cup corn kernels
1 tablespoon coconut oil
4 tablespoons vegetable oil
1/3 cup granulated sugar

Method
Put the oils into a large saucepan over a med high heat.
Add 2-3 kernels of corn.
Once the kernels start to pop add the rest of the kernels along with the sugar.
Once they start popping keep shaking the pan so that they don't burn.
Once the popping slows down quickly tip into a large bowl.
Add a few pinches of salt if preferred.

#ENJOY

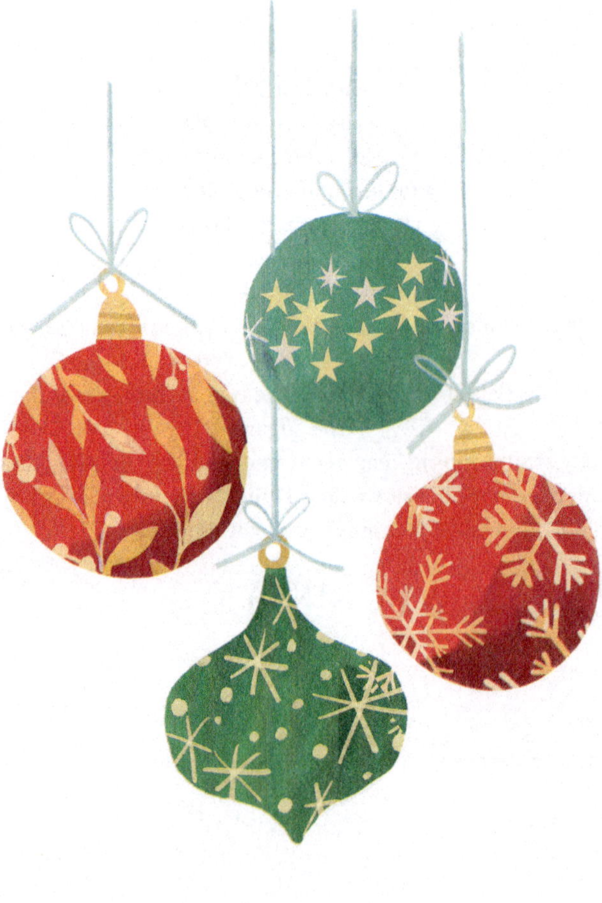

Mince Pie Crumble Bars

Ingredients
1 1/2 jars mincemeat
175g oats
200g plain flour
150g sugar
1/2 teaspoon baking powder
175g butter cold & cut into chunks

Method
Mix the oats, flour, sugar & baking powder in a large bowl.
Add the butter and rub together to form fine breadcrumbs
Pour 3/4 of the mixture into a lined tin (I used 13 x 8")
Then carefully put a thin layer of mincemeat on top.
Be careful not to dislodge the crumble mixture.
Then sprinkle the remaining crumble mix on top.

Bake at 180 for 30-35 mins until golden brown.
Leave to cool then slice.

#ENJOY

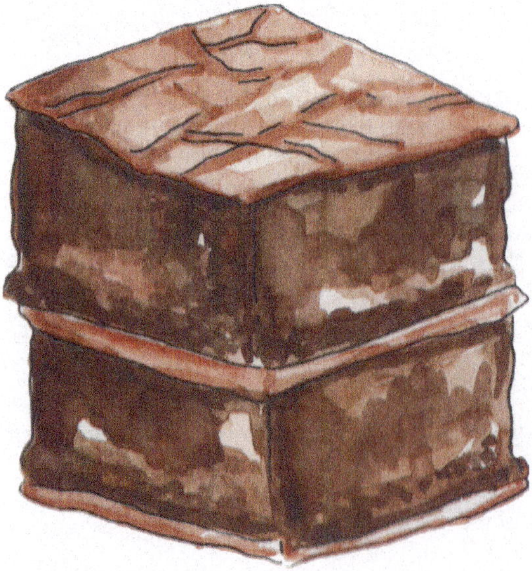

Amazing Brownies

Ingredients

70g melted butter
1 1/4 cup sugar
2 eggs plus 1 yolk
1 teaspoon vanilla
1/3 cup vegetable oil

1/8th teaspoon bicarbonate of soda
1 tablespoon cornflour
1/2 cup flour
3/4 cup cocoa powder
1/4 teaspoon salt
3/4 cup chocolate chips

Method

Combine the butter and sugar and whisk.
Add the eggs, vanilla & oil & mix.
Add the remaining ingredients and put into a lined baking tin 8x8"

Bake for 35-40 mins at 160c

#ENJOY

Best Carrot Cake Muffins

Ingredients

1 cup of vegetable oil
1 cup granulated sugar
1/2 cup brown sugar
3 eggs
2 cups self raising flour
1 teaspoon baking soda
1/2 teaspoon salt
1 teaspoon mixed spice
1 teaspoon cinnamon
1 cup buttermilk
2 cups carrots

Method

Combine the oil, sugar & eggs.
Then add all of the remaining ingredients and mix.
Spoon into 12-13 muffin/cupcake cases.
Bake for 10 mins at 200.c.
Then reduce temperature to 180 for 10 mins. Test with a skewer.
Top with a cream cheese frosting.

#ENJOY

Blueberry Filo Dessert

Ingredients

1 pack filo pastry
100ml milk
5 eggs
270ml double cream
200g sugar
1 teasp vanilla paste/extract
200g melted unsalted butter
200g blueberries

Method

Use a pastry brush, lightly butter a single sheet of filo. Concertina the sheet and roll the first one into a circle and place in the middle of a round baking dish.
Butter the remaining sheets, concertina, and place around the first sheet.
Bake in a preheated oven of 180.c for 15 minutes then remove.
In a jug briefly whisk the eggs, cream, sugar, milk & vanilla.
Scatter the blueberries around the top and in-between the filo sheets on top of the dish.
Pour the egg mixture over the filo and blueberries.
Bake at 180.c for 40 minutes or until a clean knife comes out the middle.

#ENJOY

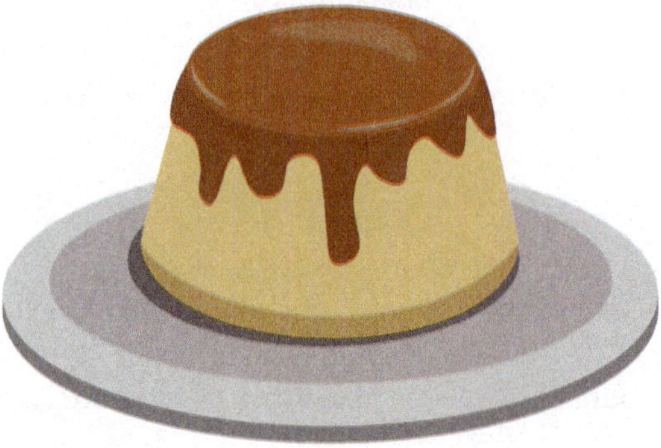

Sticky Toffee Pudding

Ingredients

150g dates chopped, 250ml hot water
1 teaspoon bicarbonate of soda

60g unsalted butter
60g granulated sugar
2 eggs, 150g self raising flour

Sauce
200g unsalted butter
400g light brown sugar
250ml double cream
1 teaspoon vanilla extract/paste

Method

Put dates and hot water in a bowl and leave for 10 mins.
In the meantime beat the butter and sugar until light and fluffy.
Add the eggs one at a time and then the flour.
Then add the date mixture.
Pour into a baking tin 8"x8"
Bake in a preheated oven 180.c for 25-30 mins or until a toothpick comes out clean.
While cake is baking melt the butter/brown sugar/cream/vanilla in a pan.
Bring to the boil and simmer for 5 mins or until a nice thick syrup consistency.
Pour over the cooked cake and serve hot with vanilla ice-cream.

#ENJOY

Printed in Great Britain
by Amazon